DOWN IN THE OCEAN

SEAFLOOR SCAVENGERS

BY MELISSA GISH

CREATIVE EDUCATION • CREATIVE PAPERBACKS

Published by Creative Education and Creative Paperbacks
P.O. Box 227, Mankato, Minnesota 56002
Creative Education and Creative Paperbacks are imprints of
The Creative Company
www.thecreativecompany.us

Design, production, and illustrations by Chelsey Luther
Art direction by Rita Marshall
Printed in China

Photographs by Alamy (imageBROKER, Suzanne Long, The Natural History Museum, Nature Picture Library, Paulo Oliveira), All-free-download.com, Creative Commons Wikimedia (Hans Hillewaert/Flickr), Dreamstime (Seadam), Getty Images (Rand McMeins/Moment, Luis Javier Sandoval/Oxford Scientific), iStockphoto (Herianus, k8thegr833, Subaqueosshutterbug, taylanibrahim, Michael Zeigler), Minden Pictures (Sean Crane, Reinhard Dirscherl/FLPA, Jurgen Freund/NPL, Scott Leslie), National Geographic Creative (Joel Sartore), NOAA (NOAA/FGBNMS/National Marine Sanctuaries), Shutterstock (Joe Belanger, Michael Bogner, David Bostock, Bill Kennedy)

Library of Congress Cataloging-in-Publication Data
Names: Gish, Melissa, author.
Title: Seafloor scavengers / Melissa Gish.
Series: Down in the ocean.
Includes bibliographical references and index.
Summary: Explore the bottoms of the world's oceans and learn about the life forms that dwell there. First-person accounts from scientists answer important questions about scavenging and parasitic creatures and how they survive.
Identifiers: LCCN 2017028052 / ISBN 978-1-60818-998-4 (hardcover) / ISBN 978-1-62832-553-9 (pbk) / ISBN 978-1-64000-027-8 (eBook)

Subjects: LCSH: 1. Marine animals—Juvenile literature. 2. Scavengers (Zoology)—Juvenile literature. 3. Ocean bottom ecology—Juvenile literature. 4. Marine ecology—Juvenile literature.

Classification: LCC QL756.5.G574 2018 / DDC 591.77—dc23

CCSS: RI.4.1, 2, 7; RI.5.1, 2, 3, 8; RST.6-8.1, 2, 5, 6, 8

First Edition HC 9 8 7 6 5 4 3 2 1
First Edition PBK 9 8 7 6 5 4 3 2 1

TABLE OF CONTENTS

WELCOME TO THE SEAFLOOR

The floor of the ocean has many similarities to dry land. There are jagged mountains and sloping hills. There are shallow valleys and deep canyons. Volcanoes spew gas and melted rock. Rich forests of life forms cover some areas of the seafloor. Other places are vast deserts. These are as bare as the surface of the moon.

The seafloor ranges from soft sand that squishes between a beachgoer's toes to the rocky floor of the Mariana Trench. Nearly seven miles (11.3 km) deep, this trench has the lowest seafloor on Earth. Scientists have explored less than 7 percent of the world's seafloor. But even in the deepest parts of the sea, they have observed animals. Many of these creatures make their living by scavenging.

■ TOTAL SEAFLOOR

■ SEAFLOOR EXPLORED (7%)

1

INFINITE WONDERS

Seafloor scavengers eat mostly detritus, or waste matter. In coastal waters, sea urchins gather up dead plants and algae. On coral reefs, shrimp nibble on scraps left over from fish feasts. In deeper waters, sea cucumbers eat fish feces. In the deep sea, scavengers eat marine snow. This drifting material may have bacteria growing on it. Many deep-sea creatures, from plankton to vampire squid, depend on marine snow.

Every now and then, scavengers receive a bountiful gift: a whale fall. This is when a whale dies and sinks to the seafloor. It can potentially feed millions of scavenger species for decades. Without scavengers, oceans would be littered with organic waste. Scavengers help keep oceans healthy.

VAMPIRE SQUID AND MARINE SNOW

Zombie worms

Osedax worms are known as zombie worms. They live on dead whale and fish bodies that sink to the seafloor. The worms attach themselves to the bones. They have no mouths and no guts. To get food, they drill into the bones. They absorb nutrients through rootlike tentacles.

Digging up dirt

Sea cucumbers are nicknamed the "earthworms of the sea." They churn up and recycle seafloor sediment in much the same way that earthworms on land do. Some species, such as warty and California sea cucumbers, are sold as food in many Asian countries.

ASK A 🐙 SCIENTIST

Are there many scavengers in the ocean?

Many animals in the oceans are scavengers, eating whatever they find, even dead things (even poop!). Many **invertebrates**, such as lobsters, crabs, shrimp, and sea cucumbers, tend to be scavengers. Even some fish are scavengers. Many scavengers are benthic, which means they live on the seafloor. There they walk (or swim) along, grabbing anything that they can find in the sediment (the "dirt" on the ocean floor).

— Dr. Kevin A. Hovel, Marine Biologist, San Diego State University

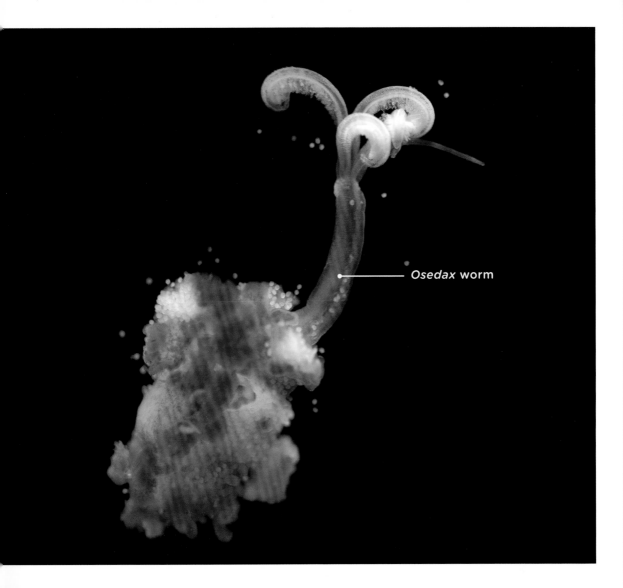

Osedax worm

sea cucumber

squat lobster

longnose spider crab

A long reach

Squat lobsters are less than four inches (10.2 cm) long. But their claws can be several times longer than their bodies. They hide in rock crevices—only their claws stick out. They scoop sediment with their claws and pick out food particles with their mouthparts.

Fancy decorations

The longnose spider crab has Velcro-like hooks on its body. It decorates itself with bad-tasting seaweed and sponges. These hold off predators as the crab combs the seafloor for waste matter. Longnose spider crabs also cling to the insides of cannonball jellyfish, nibbling food scraps and jellyfish waste.

13

ASK A SCIENTIST

What makes ocean scavengers important? Is there one that you like most?

Scavengers basically act as the ocean's recycling center. By eating up the remains of dead sea creatures, they help to ensure that useful nutrients stay in marine **food webs**. Crabs, lobsters, and even sharks scavenge for food. My personal favorite scavengers are giant isopods. They're a little creepy-looking, but they do a great job keeping the deep sea clean!

— Alexander Carsh, Marine Ecologist, San Diego State University

sea urchin

2

EAT OR BE EATEN

The ocean is filled with predators of all shapes and sizes. Some swim and overpower prey. Others set traps for unsuspecting animals. But many ocean creatures are not hunters. Instead, they follow hunters, cleaning up scraps and waste. They have senses that help them locate dead animals. They also have unique methods of eating. Most are slow-moving. They are often targeted as prey themselves. To survive, seafloor scavengers have many ways to protect themselves. Urchins have sharp spines. Sea cucumbers contain poison. Many animals rely on camouflage.

DEFENSE MECHANISMS

SEA URCHIN

POM POM CRAB

Scavenger stars

Brittle stars have 5 arms, each up to 24 inches (61 cm) long, depending on the species. The bristly arms pick up waste and carry it to the mouth. The mouth has five jaws. The stomach is made up of 10 pouches that digest food.

Eating the eaters

Coryphaenoides (*KOR-if-uh-noydz*) are a group of scavenging rattails. They swim against the current to detect the smell of dead whales on the seafloor. Sometimes, instead of eating whale blubber directly, they eat shrimp-like animals called amphipods that are feeding on the blubber.

ASK A 🐙 SCIENTIST

How do shrimp protect themselves from getting eaten?

The kinds of shrimp that we eat have small brains and simple behaviors. Nobody likes to get eaten, and these shrimp have camouflage so that they are harder to see, but they can flip their tails really quickly and shoot backwards when they are threatened. That's why the tail of a shrimp is filled with meat—it's all the muscle that flips their tails.

— Dr. Michael Robinson, Marine Biologist, Barry University

brittle star

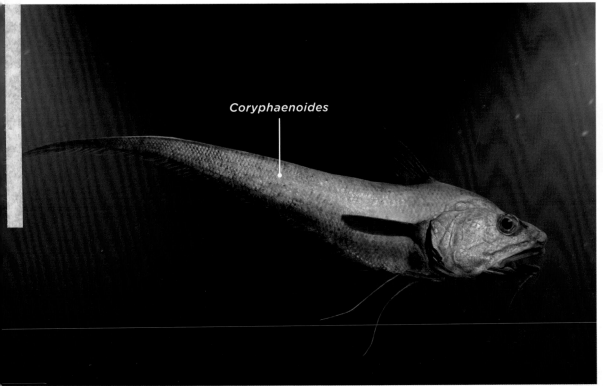

Coryphaenoides

lysianassid amphipod

Swarming scavengers

Scientists at Simon Fraser University in British Columbia once put a dead pig on the seafloor. It was protected from large scavengers by a cage. Only small amphipods could reach it. A swarm of lysianassid amphipods reduced the body to a skeleton in just three days!

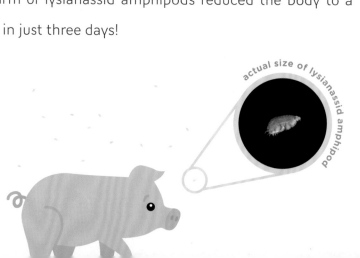

actual size of lysianassid amphipod

sea star

ASK A 🐙 SCIENTIST

Do scavengers eat pollution on the seafloor?

Yes. Pollutants often bind to ocean sediments. Scavengers can take in the pollutants from food or particles they ingest on the seafloor. Unfortunately, man-made pollutants are now even found in animals living at the very depths of the ocean—7,000 to 10,000 meters [22,966–32,808 ft] below the surface.

— Dr. Amro Hamdoun, Marine Biologist, Scripps Institution of Oceanography

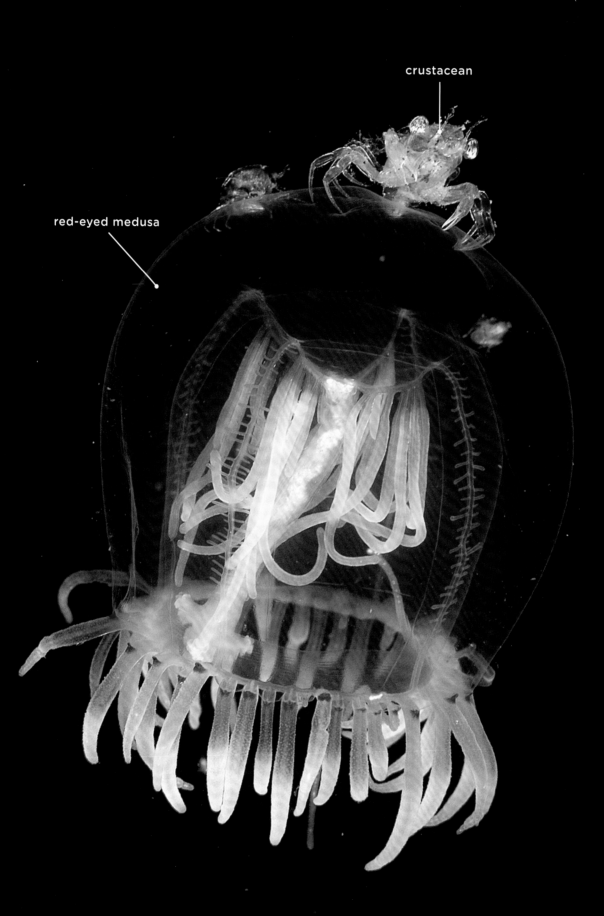

crustacean

red-eyed medusa

3

SPECIAL RELATIONSHIPS

Some scavengers stick together. Sea urchins and red king crabs gather in large groups for security. Others, such as lobsters, roam the seafloor alone. Survival is a daily challenge. Sometimes living things form special relationships to stay alive. In commensalism, one animal takes advantage of the abilities of another creature. Neither is harmed, and it turns out to be useful. Another relationship is mutualism. Partners share their abilities with each other. This arrangement gives something good to both partners. Many scavengers rely on one another.

SYMBIOTIC RELATIONSHIP EXAMPLES

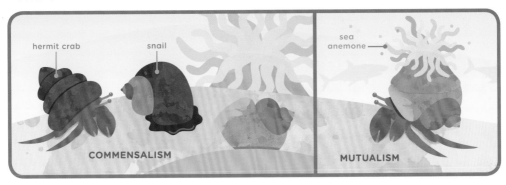

hermit crab · snail · sea anemone

COMMENSALISM

MUTUALISM

A safe ride

The brownspotted sandfish is a sea cucumber. It protects itself from predators by oozing poisonous foam. Harlequin crabs are drawn to the scent of this substance. They are not harmed. Instead, they ride on the sea cucumber, protected by its foam.

Ocean cheerleaders

Pom-pom crabs carry a small sea anemone in each claw. The anemones have stinging tentacles that carry poison. They are not bothered by most predators. The crabs help the anemones capture more food by moving them around. And the anemones protect the crabs.

ASK A 🐙 SCIENTIST

Does the ocean need parasites?

Predators and **parasites** are very important players in how natural **ecosystems** work. We might consider some of the things they do to be helpful. Some parasites might be helpful if they stop a host population from getting too large and driving something else extinct. You can say that parasites sometimes help keep a balance in an ecosystem—just like predators.

— Dr. Ryan F. Hechinger, Research Scientist, Scripps Institution of Oceanography

harlequin crab

brownspotted sandfish

pom-pom crab

sea anemone

This little piggy

Juvenile Antarctic king crabs are vulnerable to predators on the barren seafloor. Most often, they find sea pigs to ride on or hide under for as long as they can fit. The crab gets tidbits of food and protection while cleaning parasites off the sea pig.

ASK A 🐙 SCIENTIST

What makes sea cucumbers so unusual?

A sea cucumber just eats sand all day, so it doesn't need to chew anything. It has five teeth but not in its mouth. It has teeth in its butt! A small fish called the pearlfish lives inside the sea cucumber. The sea cucumber doesn't want the fish to get too big. The teeth cause the entrance to be smaller, so only a small fish can fit.

— Dr. Michael Robinson, Marine Biologist, Barry University

sea cucumber

pearlfish

horseshoe crab

4

FAMILY LIFE

The seafloor is vast. Finding mates can be difficult. This is one reason sand dollars and brittle stars live in large groups. They do not want to be too far away from potential mates. Other animals are driven to gather by seasonal instincts. Every year from May through June, horseshoe crabs gather by the millions to mate on North America's eastern shores. Male lobsters share their dens with mates for up to a week during the spring mating season. Sleeper sharks mate and then give birth to as many as 10 babies.

DELAWARE BAY

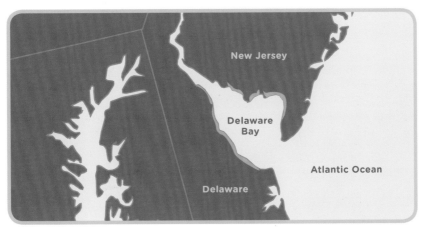

HORSESHOE CRAB SPAWNING AREA

Hanging with mom

After mating, a female red-chested sea cucumber takes her fertilized eggs out of her body. She tucks them into pouches on her skin. There they develop and later emerge as tiny sea cucumbers. Other species spew up to 130,000 eggs that hatch into free-swimming larvae.

Follow the trail

Males of the copepod species *Temora longicornis* can smell females. Also, both males and females can detect scent trails of sinking marine snow. When they catch a scent, they follow the trail to capture the food.

ASK A 🐙 SCIENTIST

Do you have a favorite ocean scavenger?

My favorite ocean scavengers are crabs. There are thousands of crab species, and many of them are scavengers. Hermit crabs live in empty shells from sea snails. They insert the back part of their bodies into the shell, which leaves their head and legs hanging out. They can retreat into the shell if they are in danger.

— Dr. Kathryn Ono, Marine Behavioral Ecologist, University of New England

hermit crab

American lobster

ASK A 🐙 SCIENTIST

Are lobsters social?

Lobsters are decidedly not friendly! You will get a painful pinch from their claw if you get too friendly yourself. As excellent food for fishes, seals, and other larger predators (as well as people), they have good reason to be defensive. They also would rather live alone than among other lobsters, except when it is time to mate. Then, some species of spiny lobsters gather in large groups.

— Dr. Jonathan Geller, Professor of Invertebrate Zoology, Moss Landing Marine Laboratories

Double life

Spot prawns begin life as males. At age two, they mate with females. Six months later, they change into females. At age three, they mate with younger males and lay up to 5,000 eggs. They carry the eggs on their abdomen for five months. Then the eggs hatch.

spot prawn

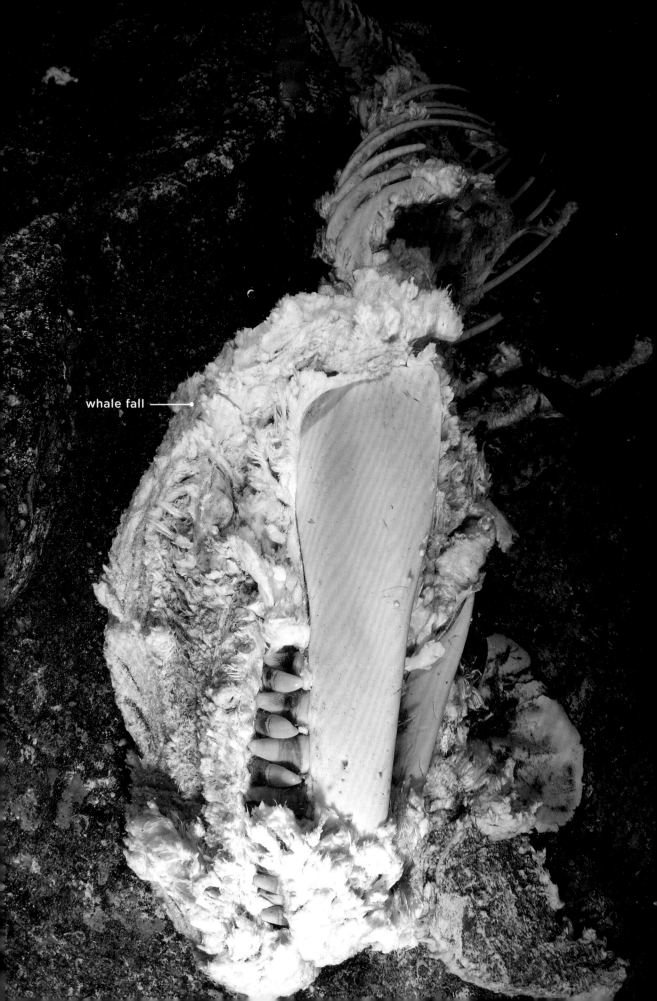
whale fall

5

OCEAN MYSTERIES

In shallow, warm water, open-sea scavengers make short work of dead organisms. Sunshine makes the flesh soggy. A floating whale can be eaten by sharks, birds, and eels in a matter of days. But sometimes animals sink where sunlight cannot reach and the water is cold. Here, dead bodies do not break down as quickly. Seafloor scavengers can feed off these meals for a long time.

Scientists began studying whale falls in the 1990s. Since then, dozens of new scavenger species have been discovered. One ongoing study is supported by the National Oceanic and Atmospheric Administration (NOAA). Scientists from around the United States collect dead whales from the sea. They sink the whales at various sites off the California coast. They monitor the bodies to learn about the various roles seafloor scavengers play in the ocean's ecosystem.

Worms in my lunch

In 2010, two new snail species were discovered off California's coast. The *Rubyspira* snails were eating whale bones more than 1.5 miles (2.4 km) deep. Scientists found *Osedax* worms in the snails' guts, too. This showed that the snails ate both the bones and the worms inside the bones.

I'm not a crab

Horseshoe crabs are called living fossils. They have remained mostly unchanged for 450 million years. They are not related to crabs. They are more closely related to spiders. They normally swim upside down. In addition to scavenging, they pull worms and mollusks from seafloor mud.

ASK A 🐙 SCIENTIST

What makes sea urchins special?

Sea urchins are able to sense their environment and move to find their food. But they have no central nervous system [a brain]! It is very hard to imagine how they do all these things. Also, at least developmentally, urchins show signs of being in a group of animals that includes both invertebrates and **vertebrates**—including humans. So that is very amazing to think about.

— Dr. James Leichter, Marine Biologist, Scripps Institution of Oceanography

horseshoe crab

sand dollar

sleeper shark

Furry cookies

Sand dollars are related to urchins. Their bodies are covered with tiny, furry spines. They move and dig themselves into sand using hairlike structures called cilia. They are called sea cookies in New Zealand. Only when they are dead and sun-bleached are their white shells revealed.

A feast for all

Sleeper sharks are fierce predators. But they are also import-ant scavengers. They bite chunks of flesh out of dead whales and large fish. This exposes soft tissue on which thousands of smaller scavengers—such as crabs, shrimp, and horseshoe crabs—can nibble.

ASK A 🐙 SCIENTIST

What are some features of hagfish?

They live at 15 to 1,000 meters [49.2–3,281 ft] and deeper. They feed on carcasses of whales and other dead animals. They don't have a lower jaw. They can tie knots in themselves. This helps them tear out pieces of flesh and also clean off their slime. They have an amazing defense mechanism involving secretion of slime that clogs up **gills** of predators.

— Dr. Martin Tresguerres, Marine Biologist, Scripps Institution of Oceanography

TRUE-LIFE SEA-FLOOR ADVENTURE

DIVING TO THE SEAFLOOR AT TORQUE SPRINGS

Malika Samsara grew up far from the ocean. But when she was a teenager, her family moved to Long Beach, California. She instantly fell in love with the Pacific Ocean. She learned to surf, snorkel, and scuba dive. One of her favorite places to dive is Torque Springs, near Santa Catalina Island. This island is about 20 miles (32.2 km) off the California coast.

One bright June morning, Malika and her friend Enid boarded a ferry at Long Beach. They stowed their gear and took seats for the hour-long ride to Catalina Island. Enid had never dived around Catalina before. Malika was looking forward to sharing the experience with her friend.

At the island, a smaller boat carried Malika and Enid to their dive spot. They donned their gear and dove into the clear blue water. Towering kelp surrounded them. It was like being in an underwater rainforest. Malika pointed downward. The rocky seafloor shimmered with color. The glossy brown shells of chestnut cowries glistened like glass pebbles on the seafloor. They ranged in size from one to nearly three inches (2.5–7.6 cm) long. About the size of a paper clip, Spanish shawl nudibranchs (*NOO-dih-branks*) are so small that they are easily overlooked. But Malika spotted one right away. She pointed out to Enid the tiny creature's bright purple-and-orange body against a dark rock.

Sea stars of all colors and sizes littered the seafloor. Nearby, a small group of red urchins had gathered to feast on some fallen kelp leaves. Creeping along a sandy spot on the seafloor was a warty sea cucumber. Malika gestured for Enid to come closer. They gently touched the sea cucumber. It felt like stiff Jell-O® under their fingertips. For more than an hour, Malika and Enid explored the kelp forest and seafloor. On their way back to Long Beach, they exclaimed to each other: "That is the coolest place on the planet!"

dredge pump ship

6

UNDER PRESSURE

The seafloor ecosystem is vital to all life in the sea. Its waste matter sustains tiny bacteria that feed small invertebrates and other scavengers. These feed larger animals up the food chain. But the seafloor is threatened every day by human activities such as oil drilling, mining, commercial fishing, and pollution.

Another problem for the seafloor comes from sediment dumping. To keep harbors and waterways deep enough for ships to travel, sediment is scooped off the seafloor. It is then dumped in other places in the ocean. This sediment, which is often polluted, buries seafloor animals and poisons their habitat. Surviving scavengers have little to eat. How humans treat the resources provided by our planet will affect the fascinating creatures that live down in the ocean for years to come.

TRAWLING

ASK A 🐙 SCIENTIST

How do human activities damage the ocean floor and animals that live there?

Human activities such as bottom trawling [dragging a heavy net over the ocean floor] for the purpose of catching shrimp and bottom-dwelling fish, such as flounder, can destroy delicate and long-lived benthic [bottom-dwelling] organisms such as sea fans, sponges, and cold-water corals, as well as other creatures. This destruction decreases the productivity and diversity of benthic organisms, and it takes many years for these habitats to recover. In some places, there is mining for minerals such as deep-water manganese nodules, and this mining is also highly destructive to benthic communities.

— Dr. Edward Carpenter, Marine Biologist, Romberg Tiburon Center for Environmental Studies, San Francisco State University

Dredging up death

Gladstone Harbor in Queensland, Australia, was dredged in 2011. Workers dumped dangerous metals in mud crab habitat. More than half the crabs studied two years after the dredging had developed a shell disease that killed them.

mud crab

brown chromis

Special seafloor sanctuary

Flower Garden Banks National Marine Sanctuary off the Texas
coast is known for its salt domes. These are stone hills formed
by minerals pushing up from the seafloor. This unique ecosystem has been protected since 1992.

ASK A 🐙 SCIENTIST

What are some human activities that harm the deep seafloor?

There are a number of threats to deep-sea animals. Fishing can reach depths of 1,500 meters [4,921 ft], and bottom trawls can damage fragile corals and sponges that live on the deep-seafloor in some areas. Deep-sea mining is potentially a threat and needs to be very carefully done to avoid causing harm to deep-sea creatures and habitats. Litter and pollution is a problem—plastics, chemicals, oil spills, and lost fishing gear can all threaten deep-sea life.

— Dr. Francis Neat, Marine Biologist, Scotland Marine and Fisheries

GLOSSARY

camouflage
the ability to hide, due to coloring or markings that blend in with a given environment

commercial
used for business and to gain a profit rather than for personal reasons

ecosystems
communities of organisms that live together in balance

feces
waste matter eliminated from the body

food webs
systems in nature in which living things depend on one another for food

gills
body parts that extract oxygen from water

invertebrates
animals that lack a backbone, including shellfish, insects, and worms

larvae
the form some juvenile animals take before changing into adults

mollusks
members of a large group of spineless animals that includes snails, slugs, mussels, clams, and octopuses

nutrients
substances that give an animal energy and help it grow

parasites
animals or plants that live on or inside another living thing (called a host) while giving nothing back to the host; some parasites cause disease or even death

plankton
algae and animals that drift or float in the ocean, many of which are microscopic

species
a group of living beings with shared characteristics and the ability to reproduce with one another

vertebrates
animals that have a backbone

SELECTED BIBLIOGRAPHY

Knowlton, Nancy. *Citizens of the Sea: Wondrous Creatures from the Census of Marine Life*. Washington, D.C.: National Geographic, 2010.

"Observing a Natural Whale Fall." Nautilus Live. https://www .nautiluslive.org/video/2016/08/03/observing-natural-whale -fall.

Palumbi, Stephen R., and Anthony R. Palumbi. *The Extreme Life of the Sea*. Princeton, N.J.: Princeton University Press, 2014.

"Sea Cucumbers." National Geographic. https://www .nationalgeographic.com/animals/invertebrates/group/sea -cucumbers/.

"Whale Falls and Whale Fall Communities." Amazing Zoology. https://amazingzoology.com/whale-falls-whale-fall -communities/.

Woodward, John. *Ocean: A Visual Encyclopedia*. New York: Dorling Kindersley, 2015.

INDEX